W9-AWN-094

The Book of Questions

*El libro de las preguntas*

# PABLO NERUDA
## *The Book of Questions*
### TRANSLATED BY WILLIAM O'DALY

COPPER CANYON PRESS

Copyright 1974 by Pablo Neruda
and Heirs of Pablo Neruda

Translation copyright 1991, 2001
by William O'Daly

All rights reserved.

Printed in Canada

Copper Canyon Press is in residence under the
auspices of the Centrum Foundation at Fort
Worden State Park in Port Townsend,
Washington. Centrum sponsors artist
residencies, education workshops for
Washington State students and teachers, blues,
jazz, and fiddle tunes festivals, classical music
performances, and The Port Townsend
Writers' Conference.

*Library of Congress*
*Cataloging-in-Publication Data*
Neruda, Pablo, 1904–1973.
[El libro de las preguntas, English & Spanish]
The book of questions / Pablo Neruda;
translated by William O'Daly.
p. cm.
Translation and original Spanish text of:
El libro de las preguntas.
ISBN 1-55659-160-8.
I. Title
PQ8097.N4L513 1991 91-72064

Copper Canyon Press
Post Office Box 271
Port Townsend, Washington 98368

Second Edition

9 8 7 6 5 4 3 2 first printing

ACKNOWLEDGMENTS

Translations from *The Book of Questions*
appeared in *Fine Madness,*
*Poetry East,* and *The Taos Review.*


TRANSLATOR'S ACKNOWLEDGMENTS

For lending his finely tuned observations and clarifications,
I remain grateful to my friend Michael Constans. Stephanie
Lutgring, with her remarkable copyediting skills, also helped
to shape the translations. To family and friends I owe a debt
that cannot be spoken or repaid. Any errors or inadequacies
are solely the responsibility of the translator.

FOR MY MOTHER AND FATHER

# INTRODUCTION

*The only true thoughts are those*
*which do not grasp their own meaning.*

—ADORNO, from *Minima Moralia*

Pablo Neruda finished *The Book of Questions* (*El libro de las preguntas*) only months before his death in September 1973. With its composition, he drinks from the common source of all his essential work, revisiting that "deep well of perpetuity" and coming full circle as an artist. These brief poems, composed entirely of questions, coalesce in the realm of paradox; they take shape in the connection between the poet's names for things and what lies beyond our ability to name. Neruda absorbed many philosophies, political doctrines, and religious creeds, he evolved through an array of poetic styles and voices, but his passion lay in improvising on essential rhythms of perception to reveal unspoken and unspeakable truths.

From *Crepusculario* and *Tentativa del hombre infinito,* two of his earliest and lesser-known works, to his late and posthumous poetry, Neruda developed a radical trust in the quest to know himself. He routinely set aside what he knew long enough to rediscover the secret, an enduring mystery, in another cadence and through other eyes. He became, as Marjorie Agosín points out, "the astute hunter," one who by *vocation* seeks "the roots of belonging" wherever he finds himself.

In *The Book of Questions,* Neruda achieves a deeper vulnerability and vision than in his earlier work, integrating in these poems the wonder of a child with the intellectual and emotional life of an adult. While he craves the clarity rendered from an examined life, he refuses to be corralled by the rational mind. To the 320 questions that compose the 74 poems of this sequence, no rational answers exist; rather, the poems present a reflective surface on which we can discern the workings of our minds and our hearts, even as each successive question opens onto the larger world.

> If all rivers are sweet
> where does the sea get its salt?

Images of rivers, sea, and salt—and in other poems, clouds, lemons, violets, friends, and enemies—all are substances or beings intertwined in our daily lives. Yet, even as they entice us to seek a reasoned answer, their tangible limits shine outward to reverberate in the Unknown. In that way, they invite us to move through our intuitive perceptions, beyond rehearsed patterns of thinking and feeling.

> Where does the rainbow end,
> in your soul or on the horizon?

These poems, submerged in not-knowing, are close to the spirit of the koan—a form of paradox that aides students of Zen in the practice of zazen, or sitting in meditation. An illustration can be found in a poem by Zen master Mumon, commenting on two monks arguing with the sixth patriarch about which is actually moving—the wind, a flag, or the mind.

> Wind, flag, mind moves.
> The same understanding.
> When the mouth opens
> All are wrong.

Ridding our daydreams of hypotheses and certainties, we become free to listen and exist where we are. We then might encounter the value of a question posed by the Sufi poet Jalâl al-Din Rumi in the thirteenth century: "How far is the light of the moon / from the moon?" And we might understand why he, after receiving no answer, turned to the moon itself and asked, "Where is God?"

*The Book of Questions* fulfills a traditional role of all the best poetry. Perhaps its greatest gift is to assist us in teaching ourselves how to perceive and sense by focusing the inner quest. When we sit, or when we "run in place" (to borrow a phrase from Roshi Charlotte Joko Beck) with images and sounds rather than flee farther into our rational minds, the imagination quietly reawakens to the possibilities of wonder and awe. In this state, we may ask our own unanswerable questions, and might come to find reflected in ourselves the world beyond mind and sight.

This unique book is a testament to everything that made Neruda an artist. He defies the imposed label of political poet or love poet, confessional poet or nature poet, and only he can rightly accuse himself of being many men, of never knowing "who I am, / nor how many I am or will be." To grasp his range, we must listen to him in his more vulnerable moments. These poems reveal much of the purity of heart that Neruda's work is known for.

> Which yellow bird
> fills its nest with lemons?

Those who have read his poems about the suffering of others at the hands of political or social pathologies will not be surprised by the lines:

> What forced labor
> does Hitler do in hell?

Neruda was a complicated artist who integrated the light with the dark and who in his highly acclaimed, fifty-year career responded to a full array of experiences, whether riding horseback over the Andes into exile, traveling the world, or happily ensconced in his seaside home in Isla Negra. Amid consistently held values, he recognized his contradictions, embraced them, and eventually freed his poetry from the confines, the dangerous simplifications of ideology and egotism. By doing so, he created a beautifully interwoven, expansive body of work.

In the ten years since the original publication of this translated edition of *The Book of Questions,* its celebration of mystery has acted as a unifying force among people of vastly varying experiences and ages. A Seattle children's theater group interpreted several of the poems in a performance for parents and friends; an experimental theater company incorporated the questions in a quasi-narrative script for one of their video productions. A Los Angeles modern dance company set several of the poems to music and movement, and one of the questions even appeared in a Hollywood feature film about a woman's struggle to complete U.S. Navy Seal training:

> When I see the sea once more
> will the sea have seen or not seen me?

These poems, moreso than any of Neruda's other work, remind us that living in a state of visionary surrender to the elemental questions, free of the quiet desperation of clinging too tightly to answers, may be our greatest act of faith. Neruda believed the inner quest was never-ending, that on some level what we learned was forgotten, so that we might learn it again.

In an earlier book, *Extravagaria,* the poet wonders:

> The sons of the sons of the son—
> what will they make of the world?
> Will they turn out good or bad?
> Worth flies or worth wheat?
>
> You don't want to answer me.
>
> But the questions do not die.

WILLIAM O'DALY
WINTER 2001

*The Book of Questions*

*El libro de las preguntas*

Why don't the immense airplanes
fly around with their children?

Which yellow bird
fills its nest with lemons?

Why don't they train helicopters
to suck honey from the sunlight?

Where did the full moon leave
its sack of flour tonight?

*Por qué los inmensos aviones
no se pasean con sus hijos?*

*Cuál es el pájaro amarillo
que llena el nido de limones?*

*Por qué no enseñan a sacar
miel del sol a los helicópteros?*

*Dónde dejó la luna llena
su saco nocturno de harina?*

If I have died and don't know it
of whom do I ask the time?

In France, where does spring
get so many leaves?

Where can a blind man live
who is pursued by bees?

If the color yellow runs out
with what will we make bread?

*Si he muerto y no me he dado cuenta*
*a quién le pregunto la hora?*

*De dónde saca tantas hojas*
*la primavera de Francia?*

*Dónde puede vivir un ciego*
*a quien persiguen las abejas?*

*Si se termina el amarillo*
*con qué vamos a hacer el pan?*

## III

Tell me, is the rose naked
or is that her only dress?

Why do trees conceal
the splendor of their roots?

Who hears the regrets
of the thieving automobile?

Is there anything in the world sadder
than a train standing in the rain?

*Dime, la rosa está desnuda*
*o sólo tiene ese vestido?*

*Por qué los árboles esconden*
*el esplendor de sus raíces?*

*Quién oye los remordimientos*
*del automóvil criminal?*

*Hay algo más triste en el mundo*
*que un tren inmóvil en la lluvia?*

How many churches are there in heaven?

Why doesn't the shark attack
the brazen sirens?

Does smoke talk with the clouds?

Is it true our desires
must be watered with dew?

Cuántas iglesias tiene el cielo?

Por qué no ataca el tiburón
a las impávidas sirenas?

Conversa el humo con las nubes?

Es verdad que las esperanzas
deben regarse con rocío?

V

What are you guarding under your hump?
said a camel to a turtle.

And the turtle replied:
What do you say to oranges?

Does a pear tree have more leaves
than *Remembrance of Things Past?*

Why do leaves commit suicide
when they feel yellow?

*Qué guardas bajo tu joroba?*
*dijo un camello a una tortuga.*

*Y la tortuga preguntó:*
*Qué conversas con las naranjas?*

*Tiene más hojas un peral*
*que* Buscando el tiempo perdido?

*Por qué se suicidan las hojas*
*cuando se sienten amarillas?*

Why does the hat of night
fly so full of holes?

What does old ash say
when it passes near the fire?

Why do clouds cry so much,
growing happier and happier?

For whom do the pistils of the sun burn
in the shadow of the eclipse?

How many bees are there in a day?

*Por qué el sombrero de la noche*
*vuela con tantos agujeros?*

*Qué dice la vieja ceniza*
*cuando camina junto al fuego?*

*Por qué lloran tanto las nubes*
*y cada vez son más alegres?*

*Para quién arden los pistilos*
*del sol en sombra del eclipse?*

*Cuántas abejas tiene el día?*

Is peace the peace of the dove?
Does the leopard wage war?

Why does the professor teach
the geography of death?

What happens to swallows
who are late for school?

Is it true they scatter
transparent letters across the sky?

*Es paz la paz de la paloma?*
*El leopardo hace la guerra?*

*Por qué enseña el profesor*
*la geografía de la muerte?*

*Qué pasa con las golondrinas*
*que llegan tarde al colegio?*

*Es verdad que reparten cartas*
*transparentes, por todo el cielo?*

VIII

What is it that upsets the volcanoes
that spit fire, cold and rage?

Why wasn't Christopher Columbus
able to discover Spain?

How many questions does a cat have?

Do tears not yet spilled
wait in small lakes?

Or are they invisible rivers
that run toward sadness?

*Qué cosa irrita a los volcanes
que escupen fuego, frío y furia?*

*Por qué Cristóbal Colón
no pudo descubrir a España?*

*Cuántas preguntas tiene un gato?*

*Las lágrimas que no se lloran
esperan en pequeños lagos?*

*O serán ríos invisibles
que corren hacia la tristeza?*

Is the sun the same as yesterday's
or is this fire different from that fire?

How do we thank the clouds
for their fleeting abundance?

From where does the thundercloud come
with its black sacks of tears?

Where are all those names
sweet as cakes of yesteryear?

Where did they go, the Donaldas,
the Clorindas, the Eduvigises?

*Es este mismo el sol de ayer*
*o es otro el fuego de su fuego?*

*Cómo agradecer a las nubes*
*esa abundancia fugitiva?*

*De dónde viene el nubarrón*
*con sus sacos negros de llanto?*

*Dónde están los nombres aquellos*
*dulces como tortas de antaño?*

*Dónde se fueron las Donaldas,*
*las Clorindas, las Eduvigis?*

X

What will they think of my hat,
the Polish, in a hundred years?

What will they say about my poetry
who never touched my blood?

How do we measure the foam
that slips from the beer?

What does a fly do, imprisoned
in one of Petrarch's sonnets?

*Qué pensarán de mi sombrero,*
*en cien años más, los polacos?*

*Qué dirán de mi poesía*
*los que no tocaron mi sangre?*

*Cómo se mide la espuma*
*que resbala de la cerveza?*

*Qué hace una mosca encarcelada*
*en un soneto de Petrarca?*

How long do others speak
if we have already spoken?

What would José Martí say
about the pedagogue Marinello?

How old is November anyway?

What does autumn go on paying for
with so much yellow money?

What is the name of the cocktail
that mixes vodka and lightning bolts?

> *Hasta cuándo hablan los demás*
> *si ya hemos hablado nosotros?*
>
> *Qué diría José Martí*
> *del pedagogo Marinello?*
>
> *Cuántos años tiene Noviembre?*
>
> *Qué sigue pagando el otoño*
> *con tanto dinero amarillo?*
>
> *Cómo se llama ese cocktail*
> *que mezcla vodka con relámpagos?*

And at whom does rice smile
with infinitely many white teeth?

Why in the darkest ages
do they write with invisible ink?

Does the beauty from Caracas know
how many skirts the rose has?

Why do the fleas
and literary sergeants bite me?

*Y a quién le sonríe el arroz
con infinitos dientes blancos?*

*Por qué en las épocas oscuras
se escribe con tinta invisible?*

*Sabe la bella de Caracas
cuántas faldas tiene la rosa?*

*Por qué me pican las pulgas
y los sargentos literarios?*

Is it true that voluptuous crocodiles
live only in Australia?

How do the oranges divide up
sunlight in the orange tree?

Did salt's teeth come
from a bitter mouth?

Is it true that a black condor
flies at night over my country?

*Es verdad que sólo en Australia*
*hay cocodrilos voluptuosos?*

*Cómo se reparten el sol*
*en el naranjo las naranjas?*

*Venía de una boca amarga*
*la dentadura de la sal?*

*Es verdad que vuela de noche*
*sobre mi patria un cóndor negro?*

And what did the rubies say
standing before the juice of pomegranates?

Why doesn't Thursday talk itself
into coming after Friday?

Who shouted with glee
when the color blue was born?

Why does the earth grieve
when the violets appear?

*Y qué dijeron los rubíes*
*ante el jugo de las granadas?*

*Pero por qué no se convence*
*el Jueves de ir después del Viernes?*

*Quiénes gritaron de alegría*
*cuando nació el color azul?*

*Por qué se entristece la tierra*
*cuando aparecen las violetas?*

But is it true that the vests
are preparing to revolt?

Why does spring once again
offer its green clothes?

Why does agriculture laugh
at the pale tears of the sky?

How did the abandoned bicycle
win its freedom?

*Pero es verdad que se prepara*
*la insurrección de los chalecos?*

*Por qué otra vez la primavera*
*ofrece sus vestidos verdes?*

*Por qué ríe la agricultura*
*del llanto pálido del cielo?*

*Cómo logró su libertad*
*la bicicleta abandonada?*

Do salt and sugar work
to build a white tower?

Is it true that in an anthill
dreams are a duty?

Do you know what the earth
meditates upon in autumn?

(Why not give a medal
to the first golden leaf?)

*Trabajan la sal y el azúcar*
*construyendo una torre blanca?*

*Es verdad que en el hormiguero*
*los sueños son obligatorios?*

*Sabes qué meditaciones*
*rumia la tierra en el otoño?*

*(Por qué no dar una medalla*
*a la primera hoja de oro?)*

Have you noticed that autumn
is like a yellow cow?

And how later the autumnal beast
is a dark skeleton?

And how winter collects
so many layers of blue?

And who asked springtime
for its kingdom of clear air?

*Te has dado cuenta que el otoño*
*es como una vaca amarilla?*

*Y cómo la bestia otoñal*
*es luego un oscuro esqueleto?*

*Y cómo el invierno acumula*
*tantos azules lineales?*

*Y quién pidió a la primavera*
*su monarquía transparente?*

How did the grapes come to know
the cluster's party line?

And do you know which is harder,
to let run to seed or to do the picking?

It is bad to live without a hell:
aren't we able to reconstruct it?

And to position sad Nixon
with his buttocks over the brazier?

Roasting him on low
with North American napalm?

*Cómo conocieron las uvas*
*la propaganda del racimo?*

*Y sabes lo que es más difícil*
*entre granar y desgranar?*

*Es malo vivir sin infierno:*
*no podemos reconstruirlo?*

*Y colocar al triste Nixon*
*con el traste sobre el brasero?*

*Quemándolo a fuego pausado*
*con napalm norteamericano?*

## XIX

Have they counted the gold
in the cornfields?

Do you know that in Patagonia
at midday, mist is green?

Who sings in the deepest water
in the abandoned lagoon?

At what does watermelon laugh
when it's murdered?

*Han contado el oro que tiene*
*el territorio del maíz?*

*Sabes que es verde la neblina*
*a mediodía, en Patagonia?*

*Quién canta en el fondo del agua*
*en la laguna abandonada?*

*De qué ríe la sandía*
*cuando la están asesinando?*

## XX

Is it true that amber contains
the tears of the sirens?

What do they call a flower
that flies from bird to bird?

Isn't it better never than late?

And why did cheese decide
to perform heroic deeds in France?


*Es verdad que el ámbar contiene*
*las lágrimas de las sirenas?*

*Cómo se llama una flor*
*que vuela de pájaro en pájaro?*

*No es mejor nunca que tarde?*

*Y por qué el queso se dispuso*
*a ejercer proezas en Francia?*

And when light was forged
did it happen in Venezuela?

Where is the center of the sea?
Why do waves never go there?

Is it true that the meteor
was a dove of amethyst?

Am I allowed to ask my book
whether it's true I wrote it?

Y *cuando se fundó la luz*
*esto sucedió en Venezuela?*

*Dónde está el centro del mar?*
*Por qué no van allí las olas?*

*Es cierto que aquel meteoro*
*fue una paloma de amatista?*

*Puedo preguntar a mi libro*
*si es verdad que yo lo escribí?*

# XXII

Love, love, his and hers,
if they've gone, where did they go?

Yesterday, yesterday I asked my eyes
when will we see each other again?

And when you change the landscape
is it with bare hands or with gloves?

How does rumor of the sky smell
when the blue of water sings?

*Amor, amor aquel y aquella,*
*si ya no son, dónde se fueron?*

*Ayer, ayer dije a mis ojos*
*cuándo volveremos a vernos?*

*Y cuando se muda el paisaje*
*son tus manos o son tus guantes?*

*Cuando canta el azul del agua*
*cómo huele el rumor del cielo?*

# XXIII

If the butterfly transmogrifies
does it turn into a flying fish?

Then it wasn't true
that God lived on the moon?

What color is the scent
of the blue weeping of violets?

How many weeks are in a day
and how many years in a month?

*Se convierte en pez volador*
*si transmigra la mariposa?*

*Entonces no era verdad*
*que vivía Dios en la luna?*

*De qué color es el olor*
*del llanto azul de las violetas?*

*Cuántas semanas tiene un día*
*y cuántos años tiene un mes?*

Is 4 the same 4 for everybody?
Are all sevens equal?

When the convict ponders the light
is it the same light that shines on you?

For the diseased, what color
do you think April is?

Which occidental monarchy
will fly flags of poppies?

*El 4 es 4 para todos?*
*Son todos los sietes iguales?*

*Cuando el preso piensa en la luz*
*es la misma que te ilumina?*

*Has pensado de qué color*
*es el Abril de los enfermos?*

*Qué monarquía occidental*
*se embandera con amapolas?*

Why did the grove undress itself
only to wait for the snow?

And how do we know which is God
among the Gods of Calcutta?

Why do all silkworms
live so raggedly?

Why is it so hard, the sweetness
of the heart of the cherry?

Is it because it must die
or because it must carry on?

*Por qué para esperar la nieve
se ha desvestido la arboleda?*

*Y cómo saber cuál es Dios
entre los Dioses de Calcuta?*

*Por qué viven tan harapientos
todos los gusanos de seda?*

*Por qué es tan dura la dulzura
del corazón de la cereza?*

*Es porque tiene que morir
o porque tiene que seguir?*

Has that solemn senator
who dedicated a castle to me

already devoured, with his nephew,
the assassin's cake?

Whom does the magnolia fool
with its fragrance of lemons?

Where does the eagle put its dagger
when its lies down on a cloud?

*Aquel solemne Senador*
*que me atribuía un castillo*

*devoró ya con su sobrino*
*la torta del asesinato?*

*A quién engaña la magnolia*
*con su fragancia de limones?*

*Dónde deja el puñal el águila*
*cuando se acuesta en una nube?*

## XXVII

Perhaps they died of shame
those trains that lost their way?

Who has never seen bitter aloe?

Where were they planted,
the eyes of comrade Paul Éluard?

Do you have room for some thorns?
they asked the rosebush.


*Murieron tal vez de vergüenza*
*estos trenes que se extraviaron?*

*Quién ha visto nunca el acíbar?*

*Dónde se plantaron los ojos*
*del camarada Paul Éluard?*

*Hay sitio para unas espinas?*
*le preguntaron al rosal.*

## XXVIII

Why don't old people remember
debts or burns?

Was it real, that scent
of the surprised maiden?

Why don't the poor understand
as soon as they stop being poor?

Where can you find a bell
that will ring in your dreams?

*Por qué no recuerdan los viejos*
*las deudas ni las quemaduras?*

*Era verdad aquel aroma*
*de la doncella sorprendida?*

*Por qué los pobres no comprenden*
*apenas dejan de ser pobres?*

*Dónde encontrar una campana*
*que suene adentro de tus sueños?*

## XXIX

What is the distance in round meters
between the sun and the oranges?

Who wakes up the sun when it falls asleep
on its burning bed?

Does the earth sing like a cricket
in the music of the heavens?

Is it true that sadness is thick
and melancholy thin?

*Qué distancia en metros redondos
hay entre el sol y las naranjas?*

*Quién despierta al sol cuando duerme
sobre su cama abrasadora?*

*Canta la tierra como un grillo
entre la música celeste?*

*Verdad que es ancha la tristeza,
delgada la melancolía?*

# XXX

When he wrote his blue book
wasn't Rubén Darío green?

Wasn't Rimbaud scarlet,
Góngora a shade of violet?

And Victor Hugo tricolored?
And I yellow ribbons?

Do all memories of the poor
huddle together in the villages?

And do the rich keep their dreams
in a box carved from minerals?

        *Cuando escribió su libro azul*
        *Rubén Darío no era verde?*

        *No era escarlata Rimbaud,*
        *Góngora de color violeta?*

        *Y Victor Hugo tricolor?*
        *Y yo a listones amarillos?*

        *Se juntan todos los recuerdos*
        *de los pobres de las aldeas?*

        *Y en una caja mineral*
        *guardaron sus sueños los ricos?*

## XXXI

Whom can I ask what I came
to make happen in this world?

Why do I move without wanting to,
why am I not able to sit still?

Why do I go rolling without wheels,
flying without wings or feathers,

and why did I decide to migrate
if my bones live in Chile?

*A quién le puedo preguntar*
*qué vine a hacer en este mundo?*

*Por qué me muevo sin querer,*
*por qué no puedo estar inmóvil?*

*Por qué voy rodando sin ruedas,*
*volando sin alas ni plumas,*

*y qué me dio por transmigrar*
*si viven en Chile mis huesos?*

## XXXII

Is there anything sillier in life
than to be called Pablo Neruda?

Is there a collector of clouds
in the Colombian sky?

Why do assemblies of umbrellas
always occur in London?

Did the Queen of Sheba
have blood the color of amaretto?

When Baudelaire used to weep
did he weep black tears?

*Hay algo más tonto en la vida*
*que llamarse Pablo Neruda?*

*Hay en el cielo de Colombia*
*un coleccionista de nubes?*

*Por qué siempre se hacen en Londres*
*los congresos de los paraguas?*

*Sangre color de amaranto*
*tenía la reina de Saba?*

*Cuando lloraba Baudelaire*
*lloraba con lágrimas negras?*

## XXXIII

And why is the sun such a bad companion
to the traveler in the desert?

And why is the sun so congenial
in the hospital garden?

Are they birds or fish
in these nets of moonlight?

Was it where they lost me
that I finally found myself?

*Y por qué el sol es tan mal amigo
del caminante en el desierto?*

*Y por qué el sol es tan simpático
en el jardín del hospital?*

*Son pájaros o son peces
en estas redes de la luna?*

*Fue adonde a mí me perdieron
que logré por fin encontrarme?*

With the virtues that I forgot
could I sew a new suit?

Why did the best rivers
leave to flow in France?

Why does it not dawn in Bolivia
after the night of Guevara?

And does his assassinated heart
search there for his assassins?

Do the black grapes of the desert
have a basic thirst for tears?

*Con las virtudes que olvidé*
*me puedo hacer un traje nuevo?*

*Por qué los ríos mejores*
*se fueron a correr en Francia?*

*Por qué no amanece en Bolivia*
*desde la noche de Guevara?*

*Y busca allí a los asesinos*
*su corazón asesinado?*

*Tienen primero gusto a lágrimas*
*las uvas negras del desierto?*

Will our life not be a tunnel
between two vague clarities?

Or will it not be a clarity
between two dark triangles?

Or will life not be a fish
prepared to be a bird?

Will death consist of nonbeing
or of dangerous substances?

*No será nuestra vida un túnel*
*entre dos vagas claridades?*

*O no será una claridad*
*entre dos triángulos oscuros?*

*O no será la vida un pez*
*preparado para ser pájaro?*

*La muerte será de no ser*
*o de sustancias peligrosas?*

# XXXVI

In the end, won't death
be an endless kitchen?

What will your disintegrated bones do,
search once more for your form?

Will your destruction merge
with another voice and other light?

Will your worms become part
of dogs or of butterflies?

*No será la muerte por fin*
*una cocina interminable?*

*Qué harán tus huesos disgregados,*
*buscarán otra vez tu forma?*

*Se fundirá tu destrucción*
*en otra voz y en otra luz?*

*Formarán parte tus gusanos*
*de perros o de mariposas?*

## XXXVII

Will Czechoslovakians or turtles
be born from your ashes?

Will your mouth kiss carnations
with other, imminent lips?

But do you know from where death
comes, from above or from below?

From microbes or walls,
from wars or winter?

*De tus cenizas nacerán*
*checoslovacos o tortugas?*

*Tu boca besará claveles*
*con otros labios venideros?*

*Pero sabes de dónde viene*
*la muerte, de arriba o de abajo?*

*De los microbios o los muros,*
*de las guerras o del invierno?*

## XXXVIII

Do you not believe that death lives
inside a cherry's sun?

Cannot a kiss of spring
also kill you?

Do you believe that ahead of you
grief carries the flag of your destiny?

And in the skull do you discover
your ancestry condemned to bone?


*No crees que vive la muerte*
*dentro del sol de una cereza?*

*No puede matarte también*
*un beso de la primavera?*

*Crees que el luto te adelanta*
*la bandera de tu destino?*

*Y encuentras en la calavera*
*tu estirpe a hueso condenada?*

## XXXIX

Do you not also sense danger
in the sea's laughter?

Do you not see a threat
in the bloody silk of the poppy?

Do you not see that the apple tree flowers
only to die in the apple?

Do you not weep surrounded by laughter
with bottles of oblivion?


*No sientes también el peligro
en la carcajada del mar?*

*No ves en la seda sangrienta
de la amapola una amenaza?*

*No ves que florece el manzano
para morir en la manzana?*

*No lloras rodeado de risa
con las botellas del olvido?*

To whom does the ragged condor
report after its mission?

What do they call the sadness
of a solitary sheep?

And what happens in the dovecote
if the doves learn to sing?

If the flies make honey
will they offend the bees?


*A quién el cóndor andrajoso*
*da cuenta de su cometido?*

*Cómo se llama la tristeza*
*en una oveja solitaria?*

*Y qué pasa en el palomar*
*si aprenden canto las palomas?*

*Si las moscas fabrican miel*
*ofenderán a las abejas?*

How long does a rhinoceros last
after he's moved to compassion?

What's new for the leaves
of recent spring?

In winter, do the leaves live
in hiding with the roots?

What did the tree learn from the earth
to be able to talk with the sky?

*Cuánto dura un rinoceronte*
*después de ser enternecido?*

*Qué cuentan de nuevo las hojas*
*de la reciente primavera?*

*Las hojas viven en invierno*
*en secreto, con las raíces?*

*Qué aprendió el árbol de la tierra*
*para conversar con el cielo?*

Does he who is always waiting suffer more
than he who's never waited for anyone?

Where does the rainbow end,
in your soul or on the horizon?

Perhaps heaven will be,
for suicides, an invisible star?

Where are the vineyards of iron
from where the meteor falls?

*Sufre más el que espera siempre*
*que aquel que nunca esperó a nadie?*

*Dónde termina el arco iris,*
*en tu alma o en el horizonte?*

*Tal vez una estrella invisible*
*será el cielo de los suicidas?*

*Dónde están las viñas de hierro*
*de donde cae el meteoro?*

## XLIII

Who was she who made love to you
in your dream, while you slept?

Where do the things in dreams go?
Do they pass to the dreams of others?

And does the father who lives in your dreams
die again when you awaken?

In dream, do plants blossom
and their solemn fruit ripen?


*Quién era aquella que te amó*
*en el sueño, cuando dormías?*

*Dónde van las cosas del sueño?*
*Se van al sueño de los otros?*

*Y el padre que vive en los sueños*
*vuelve a morir cuando despiertas?*

*Florecen las plantas del sueño*
*y maduran sus graves frutos?*

## XLIV

Where is the child I was,
still inside me or gone?

Does he know that I never loved him
and that he never loved me?

Why did we spend so much time
growing up only to separate?

Why did we both not die
when my childhood died?

And why does my skeleton pursue me
if my soul has fallen away?

*Dónde está el niño que yo fui,*
*sigue adentro de mí o se fue?*

*Sabe que no lo quise nunca*
*y que tampoco me quería?*

*Por qué anduvimos tanto tiempo*
*creciendo para separarnos?*

*Por qué no morimos los dos*
*cuando mi infancia se murió?*

*Y si el alma se me cayó*
*por qué me sigue el esqueleto?*

Is the yellow of the forest
the same as last year's?

And does the black flight
of the relentless seabird repeat itself?

And is where space ends
called death or infinity?

What weighs more heavily on the belt,
sadnesses or memories?

*El amarillo de los bosques*
*es el mismo del año ayer?*

*Y se repite el vuelo negro*
*de la tenaz ave marina?*

*Y donde termina el espacio*
*se llama muerte o infinito?*

*Qué pesan más en la cintura,*
*los dolores o los recuerdos?*

# XLVI

And what is the name of the month
that falls between December and January?

By what authority did they number
the twelve grapes of the cluster?

Why didn't they give us longer
months that last all year?

Did spring never deceive you
with kisses that didn't blossom?

*Y cómo se llama ese mes*
*que está entre Diciembre y Enero?*

*Con qué derecho numeraron*
*las doce uvas del racimo?*

*Por qué no nos dieron extensos*
*meses que duren todo el año?*

*No te engañó la primavera*
*con besos que no florecieron?*

In the middle of autumn
do you hear yellow explosions?

By what reason or injustice
does the rain weep its joy?

Which birds lead the way
when the flock takes flight?

From what does the hummingbird hang
its dazzling symmetry?

*Oyes en medio del otoño
detonaciones amarillas?*

*Por qué razón o sinrazón
llora la lluvia su alegría?*

*Qué pájaros dictan el orden
de la bandada cuando vuela?*

*De qué suspende el picaflor
su simetría deslumbrante?*

Are the breasts of the sirens
spiral shells from the sea?

Or are they petrified waves
or the stationary play of the spume?

Hasn't the meadow caught fire
with wild fireflies?

Did autumn's hairdressers
uncomb these chrysanthemums?

*Son los senos de las sirenas*
*las redondescas caracolas?*

*O son olas petrificadas*
*o juego inmóvil de la espuma?*

*No se ha incendiado la pradera*
*con las luciérnagas salvajes?*

*Los peluqueros del otoño*
*despeinaron los crisantemos?*

When I see the sea once more
will the sea have seen or not seen me?

Why do the waves ask me
the same questions I ask them?

And why do they strike the rock
with so much wasted passion?

Don't they get tired of repeating
their declaration to the sand?

*Cuando veo de nuevo el mar*
*el mar me ha visto o no me ha visto?*

*Por qué me preguntan las olas*
*lo mismo que yo les pregunto?*

*Y por qué golpean la roca*
*con tanto entusiasmo perdido?*

*No se cansan de repetir*
*su declaración a la arena?*

Who can convince the sea
to be reasonable?

What's it get from demolishing
blue amber, green granite?

And why so many wrinkles
and so many holes in the rock?

I came from behind the sea,
now where do I go when it cuts me off?

Why did I close the road,
falling into the sea's trap?

*Quién puede convencer al mar
para que sea razonable?*

*De qué le sirve demoler
ámbar azul, granito verde?*

*Y para qué tantas arrugas
y tanto agujero en la roca?*

*Yo llegué de detrás del mar
y dónde voy cuando me ataja?*

*Por qué me he cerrado el camino
cayendo en la trampa del mar?*

Why do I hate cities
smelling of women and urine?

Isn't the city the great ocean
of quaking mattresses?

Doesn't Oceania of the winds
have islands and palm trees?

Why did I return to the indifference
of the limitless ocean?

*Por qué detesto las ciudades
con olor a mujer y orina?*

*No es la ciudad el gran océano
de los colchones que palpitan?*

*La oceanía de los aires
no tiene islas y palmeras?*

*Por qué volví a la indiferencia
del océano desmedido?*

How large was the black octopus
that darkened the day's peace?

Were its branches made of iron
and its eyes, of dead fire?

And why did the tricolored whale
cut me off on the road?

Cuánto medía el pulpo negro
que oscureció la paz del día?

Eran de hierro sus ramales
y de fuego muerto sus ojos?

Y la ballena tricolor
por qué me atajó en el camino?

Who devoured before my eyes
a shark covered with pustules?

Who was guilty, the squall
or the bloodstained fishes?

Is this continual breaking
the order or the battle?

*Quién devoró frente a mis ojos*
*un tiburón lleno de pústulas?*

*Tenía la culpa el escualo*
*o los peces ensangrentados?*

*Es el orden o la batalla*
*este quebranto sucesivo?*

Is it true that swallows
are going to settle on the moon?

Will they carry spring with them
tearing it from the cornices?

Will the moon swallows
take off in autumn?

Will they search for traces of bismuth
by pecking at the sky?

And will they return to the balconies
dusted with ash?

*Es verdad que las golondrinas
van a establecerse en la luna?*

*Se llevarán la primavera
sacándola de las cornisas?*

*Se alejarán en el otoño
las golondrinas de la luna?*

*Buscarán muestras de bismuto
a picotazos en el cielo?*

*Y a los balcones volverán
espolvoreadas de ceniza?*

Why don't they send moles
and turtles to the moon?

Couldn't the animals that engineer
hollows and tunnels

take charge of
these distant inspections?

*Por qué no mandan a los topos
y a las tortugas a la luna?*

*Los animales ingenieros
de cavidades y ranuras*

*no podrían hacerse cargo
de estas lejanas inspecciones?*

You don't believe that dromedaries
keep moonlight in their humps?

Don't they sow it in the desert
with secret persistence?

And hasn't the sea been lent
for a brief time to the earth?

Won't we have to give it back
with its tides to the moon?

*No crees que los dromedarios*
*preservan luna en sus jorobas?*

*No la siembran en los desiertos*
*con persistencia clandestina?*

*Y no estará prestado el mar*
*por un corto tiempo a la tierra?*

*No tendremos que devolverlo*
*con sus mareas a la luna?*

Wouldn't it be best to outlaw
interplanetary kisses?

Why not analyze these things
before outfitting other planets?

And why not the platypus
who is dressed for space?

Weren't horseshoes made
for horses on the moon?

*No será bueno prohibir*
*los besos interplanetarios?*

*Por qué no analizar las cosas*
*antes de habilitar planetas?*

*Y por qué no el ornitorrinco*
*con su espacial indumentaria?*

*Las herraduras no se hicieron*
*para caballos de la luna?*

# LVIII

And what was beating in the night?
Were they planets or horseshoes?

This morning must I choose
between the naked sea and the sky?

And why is the sky dressed
so early in its mists?

What was awaiting me in Isla Negra?
The green truth or decorum?

*Y qué palpitaba en la noche?*
*Eran planetas o herraduras?*

*Debo escoger esta mañana*
*entre el mar desnudo y el cielo?*

*Y por qué el cielo está vestido*
*tan temprano con sus neblinas?*

*Qué me esperaba en Isla Negra?*
*La verdad verde o el decoro?*

# LIX

Why was I not born mysterious?
Why did I grow up without companions?

Who ordered me to tear down
the doors of my own pride?

And who went out to live for me
when I was sleeping or sick?

And which flag unfurled there
where they didn't forget me?

*Por qué no nací misterioso?*
*Por qué crecí sin compañía?*

*Quién me mandó desvencijar*
*las puertas de mi propio orgullo?*

*Y quién salió a vivir por mí*
*cuando dormía o enfermaba?*

*Qué bandera se desplegó*
*allí donde no me olvidaron?*

## LX

And what importance do I have
in the courtroom of oblivion?

Which is the true picture
of how the future will turn out?

Is it the grain seed
among its yellow masses?

Or is it the bony heart,
that delegate of the peach?

*Y qué importancia tengo yo*
*en el tribunal del olvido?*

*Cuál es la representación*
*del resultado venidero?*

*Es la semilla cereal*
*con su multitud amarilla?*

*O es el corazón huesudo*
*el delegado del durazno?*

Does the living drop of mercury
run downward or forever?

Will my sorrowful poetry
watch with my own eyes?

Will I have my smell and my pain
when, destroyed, I go on sleeping?

*La gota viva del azogue*
*corre hacia abajo o hacia siempre?*

*Mi poesía desdichada*
*mirará con los ojos míos?*

*Tendré mi olor y mis dolores*
*cuando yo duerma destruido?*

## LXII

What does it mean to persist
on the alley of death?

How in salt's desert
is it possible to blossom?

In the sea of nothing happens,
are there clothes to die in?

Now that the bones are gone
who lives in the final dust?


*Qué significa persistir*
*en el callejón de la muerte?*

*En el desierto de la sal*
*cómo se puede florecer?*

*En el mar del no pasa nada*
*hay vestido para morir?*

*Cuando ya se fueron los huesos*
*quién vive en el polvo final?*

How is the translation of their languages
arranged with the birds?

How do I tell the turtle
that I am slower than he?

How do I ask the flea
for his championship stats?

Or tell the carnations
that I'm grateful for their fragrance?

*Cómo se acuerda con los pájaros*
*la traducción de sus idiomas?*

*Cómo le digo a la tortuga*
*que yo le gano en lentitud?*

*Cómo le pregunto a la pulga* ·
*las cifras de su campeonato?*

*Y a los claveles qué les digo*
*agradeciendo su fragancia?*

Why do my faded clothes
flutter like a flag?

Am I sometimes evil
or am I always good?

Do we learn kindness
or the mask of kindness?

Isn't the rosebush of evil white
and aren't the flowers of goodness black?

Who assigns names and numbers
to the innumerable innocent?

*Por qué mi ropa desteñida*
*se agita como una bandera?*

*Soy un malvado alguna vez*
*o todas las veces soy bueno?*

*Es que se aprende la bondad*
*o la máscara de la bondad?*

*No es blanco el rosal del malvado*
*y negras las flores del bien?*

*Quién da los nombres y los números*
*al inocente innumerable?*

## LXV

Does the drop of metal shine
like a syllable in my song?

Does a word sometimes
slither like a serpent?

Didn't a name like an orange
creep into your heart?

From which river do fish come?
From the word *silversmithing?*

When they stow too many vowels
don't sailing ships wreck?

> Brilla la gota de metal
> como una sílaba en mi canto?
>
> Y no se arrastra una palabra
> a veces como una serpiente?
>
> No crepitó en tu corazón
> un nombre como una naranja?
>
> De qué río salen los peces?
> De la palabra platería?
>
> Y no naufragan los veleros
> por un exceso de vocales?

Do the *o*'s of the locomotive
cast smoke, fire and steam?

In which language does rain fall
over tormented cities?

At dawn, which smooth syllables
does the ocean air repeat?

Is there a star more wide open
than the word *poppy?*

Are there two fangs sharper
than the syllables of *jackal?*

*Echan humo, fuego y vapor*
*las o de las locomotoras?*

*En qué idioma cae la lluvia*
*sobre ciudades dolorosas?*

*Qué suaves sílabas repite*
*el aire del alba marina?*

*Hay una estrella más abierta*
*que la palabra* amapola?

*Hay dos colmillos más agudos*
*que las sílabas de* chacal?

Can you love me, syllabary,
and give me a meaningful kiss?

Is a dictionary a sepulchre
or a sealed honeycomb?

In which window did I remain
watching buried time?

Or is what I see from afar
what I have not yet lived?

*Puedes amarme, silabaria,*
*y darme un beso sustantivo?*

*Un diccionario es un sepulcro*
*o es un panal de miel cerrado?*

*En qué ventana me quedé*
*mirando el tiempo sepultado?*

*O lo que miro desde lejos*
*es lo que no he vivido aún?*

# LXVIII

When does the butterfly read
what flies written on its wings?

So it can understand its itinerary,
which letters does the bee know?

And with which numbers does the ant
subtract its dead soldiers?

What are cyclones called
when they stand still?

*Cuándo lee la mariposa*
*lo que vuela escrito en sus alas?*

*Qué letras conoce la abeja*
*para saber su itinerario?*

*Y con qué cifras va restando*
*la hormiga sus soldados muertos?*

*Cómo se llaman los ciclones*
*cuando no tienen movimiento?*

Do thoughts of love fall
into extinct volcanoes?

Is a crater an act of vengeance
or a punishment of the earth?

With which stars do they go on speaking,
the rivers that never reach the sea?

*Caen pensamientos de amor*
*en los volcanes extinguidos?*

*Es un cráter una venganza*
*o es un castigo de la tierra?*

*Con qué estrellas siguen hablando*
*los ríos que no desembocan?*

# LXX

What forced labor
does Hitler do in hell?

Does he paint walls or cadavers?
Does he sniff the fumes of the dead?

Do they feed him the ashes
of so many burnt children?

Or, since his death, have they given him
blood to drink from a funnel?

Or do they hammer into his mouth
the pulled gold teeth?

> *Cuál es el trabajo forzado*
> *de Hitler en el infierno?*
>
> *Pinta paredes o cadáveres?*
> *Olfatea el gas de sus muertos?*
>
> *Le dan a comer las cenizas*
> *de tantos niños calcinados?*
>
> *O le han dado desde su muerte*
> *de beber sangre en un embudo?*
>
> *O le martillan en la boca*
> *los arrancados dientes de oro?*

# LXXI

Or do they lay him down to sleep
on his barbed wire?

Or are they tattooing his skin
for the lamps in hell?

Or do black mastiffs of flame
bite him without mercy?

Or must he travel without rest,
night and day with his prisoners?

Or must he die without dying
eternally under the gas?

O le acuestan para dormir
sobre sus alambres de púas?

O le están tatuando la piel
para lámparas del infierno?

O lo muerden sin compasión
los negros mastines del fuego?

O debe de noche y de día
viajar sin tregua con sus presos?

O debe morir sin morir
eternamente bajo el gas?

## LXXII

If all rivers are sweet
where does the sea get its salt?

How do the seasons know
they must change their shirt?

Why so slowly in winter
and later with such a rapid shudder?

And how do the roots know
they must climb toward the light?

And then greet the air
with so many flowers and colors?

Is it always the same spring
who revives her role?

*Si todos los ríos son dulces*
*de dónde saca sal el mar?*

*Cómo saben las estaciones*
*que deben cambiar de camisa?*

*Por qué tan lentas en invierno*
*y tan palpitantes después?*

*Y cómo saben las raíces*
*que deben subir a la luz?*

*Y luego saludar al aire*
*con tantas flores y colores?*

*Siempre es la misma primavera*
*la que repite su papel?*

# LXXIII

Who works harder on earth,
a human or the grain's sun?

Between the fir tree and the poppy
whom does the earth love more?

Between the orchids and the wheat
which does it favor?

Why a flower with such opulence
and wheat with its dirty gold?

Does autumn enter legally
or is it an underground season?

*Quién trabaja más en la tierra,*
*el hombre o el sol cereal?*

*Entre el abeto y la amapola*
*a quién la tierra quiere más?*

*Entre las orquídeas y el trigo*
*para cuál es la preferencia?*

*Por qué tanto lujo a una flor*
*y un oro sucio para el trigo?*

*Entra el otoño legalmente*
*o es una estación clandestina?*

# LXXIV

Why does it linger in the branches
until the leaves fall?

And where are its yellow trousers
left hanging?

Is it true that autumn seems to wait
for something to happen?

Perhaps the trembling of a leaf
or the movement of the universe?

Is there a magnet under the earth,
brother magnet of autumn?

When is the appointment of the rose
decreed under the earth?

*Por qué se queda en los ramajes*
*hasta que las hojas se caen?*

*Y dónde se quedan colgados*
*sus pantalones amarillos?*

*Verdad que parece esperar*
*el otoño que pase algo?*

*Tal vez el temblor de una hoja*
*o el tránsito del universo?*

*Hay un imán bajo la tierra,*
*imán hermano del otoño?*

*Cuándo se dicta bajo tierra*
*la designación de la rosa?*

# About the Author

Pablo Neruda was born Neftali Ricardo Reyes Basoalto in Parral, Chile in 1904. During his lifetime, he served as counsel in Burma (now Myanmar) and held diplomatic posts in various East Asian and European countries. In 1945, a few years after he joined the Communist Party, Neruda was elected to the Chilean Senate. Shortly thereafter, when Chile's political climate took a sudden turn to the right, Neruda fled to Mexico, and lived as an exile for several years. He later established a permanent home at Isla Negra. In 1970 he was appointed as Chile's ambassador to France, and in 1971 he was awarded the Nobel Prize in Literature. Pablo Neruda died in 1973.

# About the Translator

William O'Daly spent seventeen years translating the late and posthumous poetry of Pablo Neruda. He has published five other books of Neruda translations with Copper Canyon Press as well as a chapbook of his own poems, *The Whale in the Web*.

OTHER BOOKS BY PABLO NERUDA
FROM COPPER CANYON PRESS

*Still Another Day*
translated by William O'Daly

*The Separate Rose*
translated by William O'Daly

*Winter Garden*
translated by William O'Daly

*Stones of the Sky*
translated by James Nolan

*The Sea and the Bells*
translated by William O'Daly

*The Yellow Heart*
translated by William O'Daly

The Chinese character for poetry is made up of two parts: "word" and "temple." It also serves as pressmark for Copper Canyon Press.

Founded in 1972, Copper Canyon Press remains dedicated to publishing poetry exclusively, from Nobel laureates to new and emerging authors. The Press thrives with the generous patronage of readers, writers, booksellers, librarians, teachers, students, and funders—everyone who shares the conviction that poetry invigorates the language and sharpens our appreciation of the world. We invite you to join this community of supporters.

PUBLISHER'S CIRCLE
Allen Foundation for the Arts
Elliott Bay Book Company
Mimi Gardner Gates
Jaech Family Fund
Lannan Foundation
Rhoady and Jeanne Marie Lee
Lila Wallace–Reader's Digest Fund
National Endowment for the Arts
Port Townsend Paper Company
U.S.–Mexico Fund for Culture
Emily Warn and Daj Oberg
Washington State Arts Commission
Witter Bynner Foundation
Charles and Barbara Wright

FOR INFORMATION AND CATALOGS:
Copper Canyon Press
Post Office Box 271
Port Townsend, Washington 98368
360/385-4925
poetry@coppercanyonpress.org
www.coppercanyonpress.org

This book was designed and typeset by Phil Kovacevich and George Lugg using Quark Xpress 4.1 on a Macintosh G4. The typeface is Sabon. This book was printed by Friesens Book Division.